Travis I. Sivart

27 Thoughts
on
Being a Villain

Travis I. Sivart

27 Thoughts on Being a Villain
27 Fictional Thoughts Series, Book 1

Cover Design by Travis I. Sivart

ISBN: 978-1-954214-51-4

Talk of the Tavern Publishing Group

Travis I. Sivart

Enjoying what you're reading?
Want more? Sign up for Travis's newsletter
and get a free book.

Go to TravisSivart.com and click on the
newsletter link on the menu bar!

Travis I. Sivart

Dedication

I dedicate this book to all those people out there who have truly outrageous and fiendish thoughts and plans, but never go through with them. And as a viewer on my live stream once said, "Get on the ball, or else risk the shame of civil service."

As a side note, I worked at the DMV for five years.

Travis I. Sivart

Contents

27 Thoughts on Being a Villain

Travis I. Sivart

Introduction

This book was an April Fools idea. On April 1st, 2023, I sat down with the folks in my live stream and suggested this concept for my next 27 Thoughts book. They loved it. They encouraged it. They showered me with gifts and threats until I started planning it with fiendish glee.

This will be written from the villain mentor's point of view. It will use coarse language, because it's written from the perspective of a bad person. It will not be graphic, but will suggest ideas that are *not* socially acceptable. If you read beyond this point, it's on you. Because villains believe in being responsible for your own choices and actions.

I now turn this over to that evil little voice in my head, but be warned, he's a snarky bastard.

Greetings, peons and pathetic petitioners of pernicious plans and projects! I am writing this book to help all of you become more like me, a villain. In this wonderful, whimsical tome of wisdom, I shall show you the basics of being the best bad bandit and betrayer of this broken society in which we reside.

I shall wax poetic and break many rules. One of those rules is content format. Travis I. Sivart, author of the previous volumes in this series, has a strict code of one thought per page, and one page per thought. I say that is a limitation, and he shan't restrict me in any way.

This book is aimed towards the modern villain, but all the ideas can be translated to fit a medieval warlord, a space tyrant, or anyone else. Unless you're an idiot, then this may be beyond the capabilities of your tiny mind and pathetic imagination.

Another rule of his is to make these books for everyone, without any offensive language. Considering I shall be discussing mischief, mayhem, maliciousness, and even murder...I poo-poo that idea. I won't be controlled by his arbitrary tenants, and shall use words such as, well, you'll see.

So, I encourage you to take notes. Just write them on the blank page next to the entry, highlight sentences directly in the pages of this book of badness, and even fold the corners of the pages. After all, we're villains and we encourage madness and chaos as often as we demand logic and strict order.

1. Origins of Evil, aka Using Your Childhood for Inspiration

Look, we all had awful childhoods in one form or another. Our early formative years were filled with domineering authority figures, bullies, and an entire society telling us how to behave and act so we fit in.

As an adult, we can rebel against that by doing what we want, all while telling others they should do what we want. Our parents don't need to be dead for that. That trope is for heroes! In fact, we can even send money home to support our dear, beloved parents. Only the best nursing home for them. After all, we can't have them living with us, can we? Not if we're staying out until all hours committing crimes. We can't have them asking where we're getting all the money for our cool things and employees when we never go to a 9-to-5 job.

Besides parents and school-age bullies, most villains' origin stories begin at the age of consent. Weird, right? Heroes all have things from before or around puberty that triggered their psychological issues—and let's be honest, they tend to have more issues than we do—but people think we made the choice to be like we are *after* we were able to vote.

In truth, villains are often those who have more vision and drive than others. We seek to better our circumstances and achieve things others never dare to dream. We come up with wild plans and ideas to change the world, and usually for the better. But I shall discuss that ad nauseam throughout this libram, and now endeavor to stay on topic.

Dig into your early years to find inspiration to propel your plans to greatness. Use that puppy that was hit by a car, that special someone who spurned your advances because you weren't cool enough to love, or even your parents, who told you would never amount to anything.

Of course, a dip in a chemical jacuzzi is always a viable impetus to the greatness of your future. But always remember to make it about yourself. We don't give up control to others for the reason we achieve the lofty goals we aim to conquer.

2. YOU Did This to Me, aka Revenge

This is an extension of the previous thought, because I am a rule breaker, and decided to discuss this age old, tried-and-true reason for doing the things we do. Revenge.

So often a hero—and I use that word with my tongue firmly in my cheek—does something that results in a person becoming something else. Or reinventing themselves because of someone else's actions. This was the case of the Joker of Batman fame, Aldrich Killian of Iron Man 3, and almost every Spider-man enemy.

It's a shame to use this as a reason for what you do, but if you use it as an inspiration to better yourself, then it is admirable. Just don't cling to the person who did it to you. Rise above it, and look down with a sneering countenance upon the bastard who threw you into a vat of acid, made you feel like a lesser person, or whatever.

The thing about revenge is the driving obsession to achieve it. It can become all-consuming and even threaten to destroy you, so it is limited in its ability to inspire. That being said, kill the smear of feces who did it and move on to bigger and better things.

After all, are you doing all the things you do for someone you hate, or are you doing it for greater reasons? Think about wealth, power, influence, and inspiring the next generation to change the world or even to just believe in themselves when no one would believe in you.

Travis I. Sivart

3. Something to Remember Me By, aka Moustache Twirling

As a villain, it is always a good idea to have a signature habit to help people remember you. The age old classic image of this would be the top hat and tails wearing landlord of old, twirling his handlebar moustache, rubbing his hands together as he stood over the damsel tied to the train tracks.

But there is so much more you can do besides a tired old cliché of a handlebar moustache! You can…eat an apple, flip a coin, twirl a pocket watch, or stroke a pussy.

Keep in mind with the last one, it also requires food, litter box, and cuddles. Scritches are of utmost importance, because if you're going to keep a pet it deserves love and attention.

It can also be a catch phrase, or—as Dr. Horrible once said—nailing the evil laugh. Joker had his various deadly smile chemicals, and Zorro had his Z shape, which he cut into everything with his sword. And don't tell me Zorro wasn't a villain, he most certainly was! He fought the establishment, stole from the government, and did a bit of rabble rousing. He and Robin Hood both.

Point being, find something small and consistent which you can include in your image. It should be special and speak to your unique style and personality.

Travis I. Sivart

4. It's the Small Things, aka You Have to Start Somewhere

When you first start out in your life of crime, you probably won't have much capital. You will need to start small, but make sure you do it with flair and panache.

You could rob a liquor or convenience store, but that's so cliché. And let's face it, we aren't here to harass the little guy. We still want to be able to pop in to pick up a liter of vodka, or a freshly rolled hot dog. After all, aren't they so delicious? For something made on steel rollers and rotated out every forty-five minutes, once you add a line of ketchup and a spicy mustard, well...yummy yummy in my tummy!

So, you need to get creative, and plan for the future. You don't want to be thought of as some D-list criminal knocking over the local spot. It only hurts the people who you rely on. Think bigger!

But not too big. Maybe an armored truck. That's still hitting a bank, you know, the faceless corporations who manipulate us into giving them our money so they make money. Or an artistic floor-to-ceiling graffiti marking the local government building. But that's not profitable, so scratch that. (I will address expenses later).

Anything you do, you want it to help build and fund your next objective. And send me your ideas. (I will address where to get ideas later).

Travis I. Sivart

5. Being Bad is a Killer, aka Murder for Fun & Profit

After all that talk of supporting your local businesses, I want to talk about killing people. Sad truth is that we are villains, and sometimes the job requires a certain amount of making people...un-living. Anti-breathing. Reverse-active. Aka, killing.

Do keep in mind once you take this step, you make enemies, and you increase the risk of facing even worse charges if you're caught. Having the insanity thing on your side so they pop you into an asylum is always a good idea, though many places have decided that insanity is no longer a viable defense.

So, if you must murder, then do it with good intentions. In other words, make sure the reward balances the risk. This can be in the profit shown. So shooting someone in a robbery is just poor sportsmanship. But knocking over a billionaire while they are on holiday and looting their vacation home...that could mean millions of dollars in profit.

Bumping off someone to stop them from supporting a new law (for example, not being able to use insanity as a scapegoat) can lead to new and exciting methods of getting out of trouble.

Always think ahead, and never let passion and emotion rule who you...un-alive.

Travis I. Sivart

6. The Mindless Masses, aka I Hate People

This is a tough one, but not really. Let's face it…the average John or Jane is super boring and usually stupid. They talk about weather, sports, or regurgitate the latest political opinion that were spoon fed from the latest meme on moronic social media.

But that means they're easy to manipulate! People are sheep, and they follow whoever shouts the loudest. It doesn't even have to make sense. There are people who still think the world is flat, and that leads me to believe—and correctly so, I assure you—they will swallow anything if presented in an engaging manner.

Tell them that someone is out to get them, or attacked someone in a minority group, and they will rally around you. They will pop up the meme-du-jour on their social media and sing your praises as a hero!

Also, they will stand around and video you on their smartphones while you blow up a building, so make sure they get a show worth them risking their lives. But also use this opportunity to let the sheep do your work. Include your message, because, after all, it's all free advertising. And there's no such thing as bad press. More on that later.

Travis I. Sivart

7. Your Health is the Most Important Thing, aka Health Plan

As a villain, you will be doing many things that are physically, emotionally, and mentally challenging. This means you need to take care of yourself.

Make sure you're getting enough sleep, proper diet, and exercise. Working out won't kill you, but being out of shape in a fight or a chase might.

Let's talk about sleep first. Sleeping at least seven hours is so important. You can't think and plot mayhem without proper rest. Make sure you turn off your phones and computers at least an hour before bed, and allow your mind to not think about all your fiendish plans.

Eating right leads to good energy levels. Sometimes when planning a heist, it's easy to swing by the drive through and pick up a grease burger. But that doesn't give your body what it needs to leap across alleys while running across rooftops. Focus on proteins and fresh vegetables, and avoid grease and carbs.

Exercise is one of the most important things you can do as a villain. They always show heroes in the movies working out. Make your own daily montage, and get that cardio in, but also build muscle. A little hand-to-hand training wouldn't hurt, either. We don't always have a henchman to take the punch for us.

And it's okay to take a "me" day, a "mental health" day, or just a few hours to watch your favorite 90s comedy and laugh a little.

Travis I. Sivart

8. Making Ends Meet, aka Expenses are Expensive

Being a villain, and an idol of millions, isn't cheap. Every job you do, you must keep the bottom line in mind. Want to use a tank to break through a bank wall or roll over innocent civilians who are marching against something? Well, that tank costs money. Just meeting the people who will sell you that tank means having to travel and making connections to add to your nefarious network.

All those things take money, and you need to create opportunities in everything you do. You see, being a great villain means being a good businessperson, as well. Sure, you can threaten some folks, but that alienates them and creates a hostile work environment. Nobody wants that, not even a villain. We want to look forward to going to work, even if that work is threatening people.

Which means knowing how to read people. Some scumbags thrive on being demeaned and abused. Hell, some folks pay extra for someone to smack them around and tell them they're a piece of shit!

Look for those people, but also look for others. It doesn't hurt to get investors. This is especially true if you're inventing new tech and weapons! They love to have the opportunity for the free publicity of a superweapon. Think how impressive it is for them to stand in the boardroom and say, "Remember that mad-scientist pulse beam that took out three city blocks? Now you can have your very own!"

On the smaller level, every person you bring onto the payroll should be out for your job. It means they will think for themselves and look for ways to increase the score.

I will offer a word of warning when dealing with organized crime. Get something on them before bringing them into the fold. They've been at this a lot longer than you, and can quickly turn the tables on you if you're not careful. So, make sure it's so profitable for them they will be loyal. Or that if they don't fall into line, they will lose something of value. That may be their reputation, their daughter, or their favorite piece of art. It's all about the same, to be honest.

Which I am not.

9. Wardrobe, aka Costumes are for Attention Whores

As a villain, you want to dress for success. Tight muscle shirts and blue jeans may be sexy on a bad boy—or bad girl, because…yum—but it's not a uniform to draw respect from your peers. You want to stand out without being ostentatious, you want your outfit to draw respect or fear, but not ridicule.

Costumes are for losers. Heroes wear costumes. Circus performers wear costumes. You are more than that. You want your outfit to draw eyes without derision. Never dress in greens and yellows, or anything that screams 1970s. Joker can pull off green and purple, but you can't. Because they will immediately think of a clown if you wear it.

A power suit is always good, business and formal or mechanical and technological. Basic black is good and simple and easy on the budget. And make sure it's tailored. Nothing makes you look more like an amateur than an ill-fitting suit.

Or if you're a warlord in a magical fantasy world, dress like it. This doesn't mean gold gilt and sparkly diamonds. Any squire would laugh at you, knowing those soft metals will collapse at the first mace bash.

Also, if you create your "work" uniform, it makes you easily recognizable and easy to dress on those mornings where you had a late night excursion and aren't feeling fashion savvy.

Travis I. Sivart

10. Hierarchy of Henchmen, aka Lackeys, Pets, & Flunkies

As a villain, you are the mastermind. Yes, you can go it alone, but let's face it…you don't want to take every bullet and punch any two-bit vigilante tosses in your direction. It's important to get a crew.

Henchmen have lots of uses. The primary one is keeping an eye out while you get your much needed—and deserved—rest. They patrol the perimeters of your hideout, go pick up lunch (or cook for you), and swing by the gun depot to get your next batch of weapons.

It's also nice to have a group of people to celebrate your successes or to help patch up a gunshot wound when needed. They are your immediate support network.

Having pets such as guard dogs or cheetahs means some extra work. They require food, housing, and care. And unless you want to walk a half dozen rottweilers and pick up massive piles of doggy doo-doo, you want henchmen. Not to mention the raw meat and the training. And who can cuddle vicious animals who attack on sight alone? You need to focus on planning and execution, let someone else take on the burden of the animals. I will stick to tickling my guinea pig. Totally not a euphemism.

Flunkies are an important part of the villain's ecosystem, as well. You can't be expected to clean up after every torture session or after a meal for yourself and a dozen guards, so make sure you get that staff who does it for you.

Travis I. Sivart

11. Diversity, aka Representation Matters

I want to take a moment to discuss something very serious and important to me personally: diversity. As a villain, we know what it's like to not be accepted by the general public. And so do many others.

It's important to show you understand that and bring in people who don't just look like you. The majority of minorities are never offered opportunities, and I think that's just...villainous. Reprehensible. Unacceptable.

If all of your henchmen are middle-class, middle-aged, white men...you're doing something very wrong. People from every walk of life have something to offer. Whether we're talking about low-income, race, gender-identity, religion, or whatever...practice diversity.

These lackeys will have a perspective—and connections—you won't. Also, come on, think about it, if you have Latino, Indian, Middle Eastern, and other people in your crew...you get an awesome variety of foods to try! If you want good tacos, that white guy isn't going to do it right. You need your guy from El Salvador to step up! Good curry doesn't come from a middle-class dude named Chad; it comes from Fatima!

Plus, let's face it...western white folks just aren't repressed and angry enough to do the violent acts against the establishment that others are excited and enthusiastic to do! I won't even go into where you can get good drugs, except pharmaceuticals. Maybe a white person could get good prescription drugs.

Travis I. Sivart

12. It's Lonely Being Bad, aka Heroes & Nemeses

Sometimes we need inspiration to go out and do the thing we want to do. Money and power aren't always enough. Sometimes we need a more…personal challenge. This is where an arch-enemy comes into play.

Now, I know I warned about revenge, and I stand by that. But sometimes it's not about that, it's about being challenged. And that's where heroes (usually self-proclaimed) and a nemesis come into play. I'd also like to point out that allying yourself or killing them is a better idea.

But if you decide you need a face to go with the thing that drives you, you have options. I recommend someone who directly opposes you, such as a vigilante. Don't choose another villain, such as a crime-lord. They are too valuable as an ally or a scapegoat to pit yourself against. And if your ego is too fragile to give someone else credit for your heinous acts, then you're in the wrong business. Pinning something on a rival is an age-old tradition that makes things more fun and exciting.

If you must have a nemesis, choose someone slightly below your skill level, which you can toy with, frustrate, and leave scratching their head. It adds another level to your villain "game" that can be very rewarding every time you outsmart them.

Travis I. Sivart

13. Being Accepted by the Public, aka Marketing & Promotion

If you're in this for the long haul, you'll want to consider your public image. Whether you're playing the political game, the billionaire industrialist, or crime lord, it's important to get the public on your side. It's crucial, once you reach a certain level, to gain the trust of the common man.

Give back to the community, support charities, and employ those in your realm of influence. If you're a petty dictator and run a small country (I'm look at you, Dr. Doom of Latveria), or a successful crime kingpin (I'm looking at you, Wilson Fisk), or a billionaire genius (I'm looking at you Lex Luthor and Elon Musk), you need a good public relations manager.

Small neighborhood events are always good if you're not on those levels. Buy a council member, support the high school fundraiser, and get your name on the local library support wall.

But more importantly, always remember the power of social media! Becoming an influencer is something anyone can do nowadays! Post those things you want people to think and remember. Tell them how great you are. Criminal masterminds have won presidencies this way.

You do need to be careful, though. The public loves to turn on their idols, so this can be a double-edged sword if you get pulled into the spotlight for something you did wrong.

Travis I. Sivart

14. Politics & Politicians, aka Getting Dirty is Icky

Speaking of politics, ugh, it's a necessary evil in the villain profession. You can go into it yourself, but it is super draining and time consuming. But supporting a campaign—preferably through a mouthpiece and from the shadows—can give you a lot of leverage when things get rough.

If you're pulling a job and spending a lot of money to get the gear, spend a little extra to create a "wag-the-dog" campaign. A hard-hitting news story of corruption, a club incident, or just a good, old-fashioned scandal can go a long way to misdirect public attention from your shady deals.

Politicians are also a great scapegoat. If you get busted buying weapons, pointing a finger at a corrupt official takes almost all the blame and attention off of you.

Travis I. Sivart

15. Public Appearances, aka How to Make an Entrance

As a villain, you want people to clear the floor when you come out to dance. This can be for anything from a gala ball to a street battle. It takes some prep work in some cases, such as the PR I mentioned before, or a string of infamous acts so people want to watch but not interfere. Your outfit is important here, recognizable but cool, as I mentioned before.

You can't just wander in unless it's behind your nemesis while they're on stage making a speech. You want to really have a "wow" factor built in. Fireworks—though not necessarily literal—should draw all eyes to you.

If you're the more boots-on-the-ground sort of villain, then an exploding brick or cinder block wall is good. If you're the corporate type, entering in a finely tailored suit into a boardroom, then timing is your fireworks.

I'll tell you one thing that never fails is descending from above. Whether in the street, or literally breaking through the ceiling of an office building, it gets attention. Keep in mind the expenses of collateral damage if you own the building, though.

The real trick is doing it with panache and style. Attitude is seventy percent of an entrance, your outfit is twenty percent, and the rest is what you say once you have all eyes on you. Don't go into a situation without a relevant and pithy comment ready. I recommend having a few things rehearsed, then tailor it to the situation.

Travis I. Sivart

16. Volcanos & Penthouses, aka Building a Reasonable Lair

Your home base is ultimately important. It's the outward expression of everything you've done and everything you hope to achieve. There's nothing wrong with working out of a warehouse, but it doesn't scream successful and moving up. It kinda mutters street-level thug who can't do any better.

You also don't want a penthouse apartment if you're housing twenty thugs and a dozen pit bulls. Your henchmen would spend more time in the elevator to walk all the dogs, then planning the next caper. I think we'd all love a tropical island with an impressive volcano erupting in the distance, but really...you're on borrowed time then, and just begging for a natural disaster.

You have to consider commute time and distance for your activities. If you don't have something close to where you operate, you need bolt holes, hideaways, and resupply depots. All those things add to expenses.

Setting up in an apartment or suburbia also encourages bored and nosey neighbors to track and report your movements.

So, where do you set up your base of operations?

Strip malls, with housing nearby. A front business is fine and keeps suspicion away. They tend to be less expensive, and an easy smoke screen for comings and goings. A vape shop is wonderful, and provides reasonable recruitment possibilities, and everyone else generally doesn't care what's going on if they can get their CBD gummies and glass pipe. Neighbors are used to glassy eyed or shifty people coming and going.

Another business option, if you have guard dogs, is a grooming shop. But in either of these cases, there are challenges to face.

If you are financially independent, then a warehouse is now a good idea. It can look like nothing on the outside, but still be fancy and appealing on the inside. Industrial complexes can also be used in this instance, allowing trucks to come and go, and a variety of "workers" to rotate through. Most of these two things can have a full kitchen, restroom facilities, and even sleeping quarters, if needed.

I do recommend, whatever you choose, have your own private place of residence. A place away from your stock henchmen, something only your most trusted people know about, allows you to feel secure in case some low-life criminal you hired gets ideas.

17. They Poop and Whine, aka The Care & Feeding of Prisoners

I hate kidnapping or holding prisoners. It adds multiple levels of where things can go wrong. A flunky can get an attack of conscience and turn you in or try to set your prisoner loose, plus you got to feed the captive and provide sanitary needs.

Your living merchandise also talks. And oh my god, do they talk! They never shut up! Whining, crying, begging, pleading, bargaining, all day long. It's not like in the movies where you get to walk in, say your threatening piece, and leave. They make it all about them and their needs, their comfort, their family, and so on. It's super annoying.

And if you don't have a toilet in the room with them, then you have to give them a bucket or a chem toilet, and someone has to clean it. Or you have to let them out to use the potty. And if they're over forty, or under thirteen, they have to go so many times a day. It's like they're made of piss and shit.

Look, just don't do it. Avoid a captive like the plague, because that's exactly what they are…an itchy, scratchy, irritating pile of whining.

Travis I. Sivart

18. Your Idea is My Idea, aka Get Inspiration Where You Can

I am—in case you are completely oblivious and haven't noticed up to this point—a villain. And this tantalizing tidbit of tumultuous insight is all about connecting with your inner scoundrel. If you are fresh out of ideas in your little head, then dig into the person next to you.

Now, I don't mean doing it physically and in actuality, no matter how satisfying that may be. I mean, you should engage them in conversation and appear to be intrigued, impressed, and interested. Get them to free all those well-thought out plans into the room the two of you are sharing, and then bash their skull in if it is what you still desire.

Sometimes we hit a dry spell, and we need to look around us for something new and fresh, original and creative, or perhaps…just something to do we didn't think of ourselves.

Use your friends, family, colleagues, or flunkies to provide the font of inspiration when you are in a dry spell. Even your enemies can assist when you have a rough patch. Their suspicions and accusations can trigger that inner villain to rise up—with a maniacal cackle—and move forward with confidence and authority.

So, whether it is the Girl Scout staring up at you with those big, doe-like, brown eyes, or the hardened glare of your nemesis, don't toss aside a good idea just because you didn't think of it first. Kill them, dispose of the corpse, and move forward to claim the genius plot as your own!

19. Gadgets & Gizmos, aka Tech is a Pain in the Ass

Nothing is more delightful than a fully automated effect. That may be a doomsday countdown, a killer bot, or just your stupid-ass smartphone. But one thing I can guarantee about a computer is that it will fail you—or be hacked—at a critical moment.

And can we discuss that for a moment? Of course we may, because this is my book and I shall do as I like.

Technology can be a wonderful thing, but simple mechanical things are more…definitive. A catapult will fling something more often than a mechanized monstrosity with apps and programs. Also, the cost of the former is much more reasonable than the latter.

Also, flunkies can pull a lever so much easier than typing in a command. Sound silly? Well, it is. The issue with tech employees is that they're smart, and that often means they have their own plans, ideas, and can often attempt to turn on you to usurp your momentum.

Sigh…this all means, don't trust technology. A simplification is that the more moving parts, the more something can go wrong. A sledge hammer is more reliable than a computerized monstrosity to do the same task.

Travis I. Sivart

20. Tricks & Traps for the Win, aka Kill Them Without Being There

Now, considering the previous discourse in the last chapter...there is a beauty and grace in destroying your opponent in a physical trap of your design. Whether it be a laser while the disillusioned do-gooder is strapped to a table, or an elegantly simple rock slide, these traps can tickle your fancy and provide a much needed distraction to the doldrums of your vile plot.

And plots do get dull, believe or not. It's not all fun and games, even if you designed it that way. But, chin up, and keep your eyes on the prize...killing the meddling kids who would reveal your machinations before you are ready for such a revelation.

In your lair, traps can be invaluable. Line the main entrance, the obvious way in, with deadly darts, pernicious pitfalls, and hidden hinks. Point is, don't let a moron into your lair or the latest place you have designs on conquering. That means that you need an employee entrance for all the henchmen, but still toss a few surprises in.

A word of warning: if you design a trap, then you must know if it needs to be attended in the springing of said surprise. Walking away when James Bond is watching the laser beam approach his massive man bits only allows him to escape unobserved. Instead, enjoy the experience, and if he breaks loose, shoot the bastard in the head.

Traps should be an extension of you and represent you in a way that nothing else can. Don't overextend, but allow any traps to be a fluid representation of your own unique personality.

Travis I. Sivart

21. Broken Promises, aka Stabbing Your Buddy in the Back

Sometimes it is necessary to have an accomplice or even a partner. But the sad fact is, this cuts into profit. That doesn't mean they can't be of immense use. The trick of this is to make them feel they are in charge, when in fact you are just setting them up to take the fall...or the bullet of the over-compensating idiot who thinks they can stop you.

Trust me on this, if you aren't planning to betray the person standing beside you, then you are short-sighted. Because they are definitely waiting for the perfect moment to toss you to the wolves. They don't want to share the spoils with anyone, and most assuredly were plotting for the perfect moment to flip the script and take everything you've worked so hard to bring to fruition!

Make your deal, sign a contract—which is idiocy at its best among villains, like they're going to take you to court?—or whatever needs done to recruit the help you need. But, plan for that perfect moment to stab them in the back.

That may be as a patsy, or when they are doing a stupid fist pump when you killed your opposition, or just poisoning them at the really long dining table while raising a celebratory flute of champagne.

Contingencies are the key, and planning for them. Every person you interact with is a tool, and tools lose their effectiveness and need in time.

22. Monologuing, aka Explaining Your Fiendish Plan to Idiots

Monologuing is for idiots and amateurs. If you need the kind of mental and emotional support from your enemy by monologuing, then you're doing something very wrong. You're a weak, stupid, and...ugh, moronic individual! Unless...you're holding a gun to their head with your finger on the trigger, and pull it a moment before you explain your plan.

Look, I get you want the world to know you're a genius, but come on...if they can't figure out why and how you're doing all the things, then you did it right! Explaining all the things seconds before you achieve all the things is so needy. You just want confirmation from the one person you should care least about.

Don't be that guy, or gal, or person, who can't live without one upping your adversary. It's pathetic. It's an embarrassment. Be your own person without needing the approval of the person who is looking for any reason to stop you and your incredible drive and effort to change the world!

If you really need to spill every detail of your plan, find a drinking buddy. Get a pet. Or, at the very worst, reveal all the details to your army of minions after accomplishing your plan.

Then kill them all, because they *will* use that shit against you later. Except the pets, never kill an animal. Everyone will turn on you if you do that.

Travis I. Sivart

23. Making an Exit, aka The Getaway

Entrances are important, but a good exit is more important! Always have a way out, because the heroes are in it for hell or high water. They aren't leaving. They will try to stop you at all costs.

In any engagement, have an exit strategy, and be prepared to do it in style, like it was *your* idea, because it will be! Prepare for contingencies, and I speak from experience.

You know, this one time, I was in a crowd in a very well-known city…right in the center of all the cops and people. I had five stupid people who were gunning for me, and I had three outs. A helicopter, a back alley, and gas canisters waiting to pop in a series of smoke and explosions. Point is, I didn't "win" that encounter, but I did get away.

Always have multiple outs, and in the meantime, do the deed you came to do while resting easy on knowing you will leave in one piece, no matter what happens.

Travis I. Sivart

24. Flipping the Tables, aka Being Good

When doing what most people would consider reprehensible, it's easy to surprise them. Also, this ties into the PR side of things. If you can show what you're trying to achieve and reveal the lies of the powers that be, then suddenly you can become the good guy and the hero.

Do you think Robin Hood was a villain? No, you thought of him as the hero! Same for Zorro. Both these figures fought against the trusted government, and that's what we're doing, correct?

So, why not work that distrust of the system into your plan? People are wired to distrust people in power, and if you can show how you are trying to change the system to work for everyone…then how can anyone doubt you are working for their best interests?

This makes it harder for anyone who tries to stop you from discrediting you. You've already pointedly declared that you are against the current regime and rule. You are the hero, trying to make a difference and open up opportunities, looking out for the little guy, and turn the tables.

Once you get the populace on your side, then it is a short journey to ruling them all with their complete support and backing!

Travis I. Sivart

25. World Domination, aka You're an Idiot

Ruling the world is a beautiful dream, but complete crap. First, it's a whole lot of time with everyone whining about how they would do it differently. You have entire countries working against you, and the individual in any educated nation will cry about the evil of a world government.

It's a madman's fantasy to think he can get everyone to agree with the concept of all the peoples of the planet living together and striving for a common goal of advancing the race.

People thrive on fearing one another, knowing with all confidence that they are special and right. That their way is the right way, and they are terrified of having to change, even if the benefits outweigh everything else.

It's much better to choose a small group, convince them that your ideas match their own, and let them do the work for you.

Really, though, do you want to rule the world? It's so much work, with so many tiny groups of vocal people who get all the attention because of social media. Do you really want to struggle against the rationalization of thousands of splinters, or would you rather just focus on making money and living the good life?

Travis I. Sivart

26. What's Next? aka Planning Ahead

Every plan, caper, and heist should work towards your larger plot. Every crime you commit should fit into the greater scheme, otherwise why are you even a villain?

You should have an endgame, retirement, and hopefully at a young age while you still have your health and (sometimes questionable) sanity to enjoy the fruits of your labors. Also, you want to go out on top, not rotting in prison.

We've already discussed how you start, but where is the finish line for you? This is an important question. Otherwise you could end up as a crazy old coot who isn't even allowed on Twitter (or X, or whatever) anymore.

Returning to the point, plan ahead. You don't need years of dastardly, twisting, and maniacal schemes cooked up with every detail mapped out. But like a road trip, you do need milestones and major stops in mind. Details are for the next item on your nefarious list, but a long-term concept is helpful in making sure you're not just spinning your rancorous wheels.

Common people think they finish high school, go to college, and get a high-paying job to work in until retirement. They want to find someone to share that with, maybe squirt out some crumb snatchers, and have a circle of friends to celebrate their successes as they happen.

It's not so different for a villain. You start with the little jobs to get working capital, move to larger jobs, find a partner, get some henchmen, and network, so you have other recidivist types to cackle about your schemes with!

Travis I. Sivart

27. Whimsey, aka Always Have Fun

The bottom line is to do what you love and to love what you do. As some idiot said, if you love what you do, then you'll never work a day in your life. He said that right before I took everything he owned. He's working now, trying to recollect his hard-earned wealth, which is now mine.

It's important to stop and smell the flowers. Being a villain isn't all about torture and mayhem. After all, why steal priceless works of art and gems if you don't display them and take time to appreciate your ill-gotten booty?

Find a flunky that tells dad jokes. Laugh with them, and when they get annoying, kill them. Then you can tell the jokes and your minions will laugh along with you…even if they don't find you funny, because you just killed a guy for the comedy gold of puns.

If you find you're constantly stressed by robbing banks or hacking government installations, then switch it up a little. Try knocking off a drug kingpin of a small country. It's exciting and profitable. Or hit a museum. They always have something pretty to add to your collection.

But most important is surrounding yourself with people who adore you and always tell you how great you are. You might even mentor younger villains, and then—like a pyramid scheme—take part of their profits, and take some pride in watching those little malcontents commit baneful atrocities. Scrapbook those moments, and create something you can look back on and smile. Scrapbooking is fun.

But always rig your lair to self-destruct. All these things leave a trail of evidence, and that can ruin everything.

Enjoying what you're reading?
Want more? Sign up for Travis's newsletter
and get a free book.

Go to TravisSivart.com and click on the
newsletter link on the menu bar!

About the Author

Travis I. Sivart is a prolific author of Fantasy, Science Fiction, Social DIY, and more. He's created The Traverse Reality, a shared universe that connects his cyberpunk, fantasy, and steampunk worlds, with characters readers love.

Travis I. Sivart has been writing and telling stories since he was a young child. Perhaps it was inevitable he would call grappling with words and language a career—and loving every moment. He's privileged to share his work with a large and welcoming audience. Get in touch to discover more about his work, writing process, and future endeavors.

You can sometimes find him live-streaming the writing and editing of his latest project from his home in Central Virginia, surrounded by too many cats.

You can get a free book, and discover Travis's other series, podcasts, live-streams, social media, and more at www.TravisSivart.com.

Travis I. Sivart

If you enjoyed this book…

Please let others know by reviewing it on Amazon or Goodreads, and let others know your thoughts!

Other books by Travis I. Sivart:

The Portals Series
What if you died and woke up in a new world and in a new body? Three strangers from our world awaken in a world of spells, dragons, and elves in the aftermath of an apocalypse.

The Silver & Smith Chronicles
Silver, a billionaire bounty hunter, joins forces with Henrietta "Hank" Smith to find mystical artifacts in a race against criminals and corporations in a dystopian, cyberpunk world with a dash of pulp noir. Join their ongoing adventures of cyberpulp!

Journal of a Stranger, Volume I & II
The thoughts, ideas, philosophies, and inspirations of a time traveling adventurer. Delving into the psychology of man, life's eternal questions, burning passions, and the quirky pseudo-science of his mind, and more.

The Downfall Series: Harbinger
The Talisman came again, but this time it didn't leave. The magical emanations of the comet have brought terrors from the bowels of the earth and increased the powers of an insane necromancer. The chaos above brought out others seeking to wrest control of the land. Five people from different walks of life are thrown together by these events with the knowledge that the world as they know it is ending.

27 Thoughts on Being a Villain

Travis I. Sivart